I0390540

WordPress

How to Build a WordPress Website & Generate Web Traffic With Perfect SEO

Double Book Bundle

Arnold De Vries

Copyright © 2017 by HHB Solutions
All rights reserved

This document attempts to provide exact and reliable information regarding the topics and issues covered. If advice is necessary, legal or professional, a practiced individual should be ordered. No part of this book may be reproduced in any form or by any electronic or mechanical means, including information storage and retrieval systems, without explicit permission in writing from the publisher or writer, except by a reviewer who may quote brief passages in a published review.

The information provided herein is stated to be truthful and consistent, in that any liability, in terms of inattention or otherwise, by any usage or abuse of any policies, processes, or directions contained within is the solitary and utter responsibility of the recipient reader. Under no circumstances will any legal responsibilities or blame be held against the publisher for any reparation, damages, or monetary loss due to the information herein, either directly or indirectly.

This books makes no guarantees of success or implied promises. Any type of strategy detailed in these pages can work or has worked for others, but results will vary based on individual efforts and circumstances.

1st Edition, January 2017

WordPress

Beginners Guide to Starting a WordPress Blog or Website from Scratch

Book 1

Arnold De Vries

Table of Contents

Chapter 1:

Introduction

If you're reading this, you must be ready to start your own blog or website and delve into the exciting world of online content. More likely, you want to get started with making money online, and you're possibly looking to start your own online business. In this day and age, it has become ever more important that you create your own strong online presence as a business. This WordPress guide will teach you all about getting started with that!

Building a website used to be a complicated and lengthy endeavor. Luckily, there now are many solutions for starting a website within hours, sometimes even minutes. It should be no surprise that I'm trying to introduce you to website building using WordPress. WordPress is one of the easiest tools you can use to get started in your online adventure. Many millions of websites have been built using this tool, and yours will likely be joining them soon.

Basically, WordPress is an open-source content management system. It is one of the most powerful systems or tools available online today, with a user base of literally millions of people. These are people that probably don't even have clue about the complicated HTML-coding language that is used to build sites.

Utilize this book to help you make sure you are ready to take on your WordPress adventure. You will learn from the beginning what steps you need to take to create and run a successful WordPress website. No prior knowledge required. If you do have some knowledge already, then great, you have a head start!

This in-depth guide will help you navigate through the jungle of WordPress themes, plugins, setting and many other useful features to optimize your site. So, starting from nothing, let's get that website going. The following chapters will help you get started with ease.

Chapter 2:

The Basics of WordPress

What might come natural to some, others will find confusing. So let's start with the basics. What exactly is WordPress and why should you use it?

What is WordPress?

WordPress is professionally known as a Content Management System (CMS); this means that this tool gives users the ability to create and modify digital content on a common user interface. Or to say it the language of a normal human being: WordPress is a tool to make websites. It enables you to develop your blog and website, edit it, add your own content, and publish it on the internet.

The process of creating a website can be quite intimidating for someone who has never done this before. However, WordPress enables you to build a website, even when you do not have any knowledge on HTML-code or other technicalities. You're guided in every step by the many thousands of plugin-software tools. And no, this will not cost you a single dollar. That's right, using WordPress is as cheap as it gets... $0,00!

Is WordPress free?

Yes, WordPress is free! When you take advantage of just the free stuff, you get a lot of really awesome and helpful tools. That's what this guide is here to teach you: how to take advantage of all of these awesome features that WordPress has to offer. WordPress does have some other paid options as well. You can pay for themes and other tools, but it is not required. And it is certainly not recommended to get paid software plugins for your website when you're just starting out.

This guide will also examine some of these paid options and the scenarios in which you might want to pay for some other services rather than just rely on free features. Should you chose to purchase these options? This guide can help you learn which options to purchase, as well as how to make the right purchase for your website.

For example, if you chose to purchase a theme, make sure you carefully test that theme in multiple scenarios and consider all options before you purchase. The last thing you want to do is purchase a theme that ends up not working for what you need and want. Generally, it is highly recommendable to start off with a WordPress theme that is completely free.

Why is WordPress preferred?

WordPress has a lot of really awesome benefits that give you a good reason to use them. Today, WordPress powers over 60,000 websites, and they didn't get there by chance. WordPress offers over 19,000 *free* plug-ins to help you optimize and customize your site. It is open-source, so these plug-ins get added to by software developers around the world daily. WordPress provides an elegant and easy to use platform that is constantly being updated for the better. WordPress is not the only option available to you; the internet is full of different hosting tools and content management systems, but WordPress provides a highly superior experience to you. WordPress is easy to use, has tons of customize options, and has more users and more developers than any other CMS platform.

WordPress is not only free, but it is high quality free. There will always be trade-offs for selecting a free service over a paid one. This is an example that is reiterated constantly throughout our lives. Even if we want to play a 'free' game on our phones we often have to choose between ads and extra payment. Just like with applications, there is a tradeoff associated with choosing a free version over a paid version. However, WordPress is not like the other free websites.

It is easy to prefer WordPress when you recognize the quality of what you are getting. WordPress is easy to use and learn, helpful and intuitive, and it comes with and awesome community of other WordPress users. WordPress can offer you strong analytical, creation, and functioning tools. The biggest issue with WordPress, is learning how to take advantage of all that it has to offer:

- How do you use it?
- How do you make the best website?
- How do you get started and how do you finish?
- What theme do you pick?
- How do you customize it?
- What software plug-ins are available?
- How do I utilize these plug-ins to my advantage?

- What do I need to do to put the best website out there?

These are all things you will find yourself asking as you work on your new WordPress website, and these are the things that this book will help you with. WordPress is an endless fount of resources and possibilities. Get ready to take advantage of one of the strongest websites the internet has to offer.

Chapter 3:

Hosting and Domain Names

The first step to getting your website set up is to actually get your website linked up to a server. There's tons of cheap hosting services out there that will help you on your way with this. Furthermore, you will need a website domain name, which is the webpage that gets displayed in the URL-bar of your browser. Let's examine both of these essential steps in detail.

Where to get Hosting

Choosing a host in an important part of your WordPress site experience. There are hundreds of thousands of hosts available through the internet. Having this many options it nice, but you want to make sure that you select the correct one. You want to find a good balance between cost efficiency and quality. Find a host that you know will work well with the WordPress software. *Remember*, you only need to find a host if you have downloaded WordPress from WordPress.org. If you are utilizing the free set-up from WordPress.com, you do not have to find one; WordPress.com will be your host for you.

WordPress.org does have a few hosts that they personally suggest. These can be found at https://wordpress.org/hosting/. Do not think that these are the only hosts you are limited to. There are thousands of hosts that are compatible with WordPress. Every site is different, so every host is different. You will want to find the one that is best for you. Usually, for beginners it is better to choose a cheaper hosting service like HostGator. If you know you are going to make more than one website, I highly recommend you choose the Baby Plan (the medium option, not the cheapest), since the Hatchling plan only supports a single domain.

The WordPress software has a set of minimum requirements. These requirements can be found at https://wordpress.org/about/requirements/. As long as the host that you choose meets these minimum requirements, it should work with WordPress. When you use a WordPress recommended host, however, you are using hosts that WordPress has tested that knows works well with the software. This is important information to pay attention to. Choose the right host for your website. Selecting the wrong host may create problematic issues for your website that you should not have to worry about fixing.

Choosing Your Domain Name

Choosing a domain name is especially important. Your domain name is your identifier. It is the name that everyone who visits your website will type into their address bars. Choose your domain name carefully and check it to make sure it is not already taken. Here are some important tips you must remember as you select your domain name.

Make it unique and memorable

You do not want to be mistaken for another similarly worded site. You do not want those visitors to go to another site instead of yours. You also do not want to be boring.

You want those visitors to remember where they viewed the fantastic content that you present and go back to see more: time and time again.

Make it short

Do not make your domain name too long, you will, again, deter the visitors. You will make your site difficult to work with and promote. Some very short domain names are so-called 'premium names'. These can only be bought for large sums of money. It is recommendable to only choose a domain name that you can buy and register for cheap (around 10 dollars per year).

Check for availability

People buy and register domain all the time. Most regular .com names are already taken, so you need to actually check if the domain name of your choice is still available for sale, or if someone already beat you to it. You can check this by simply going to a domain name registration service (such as NameCheap), and type in a few website names you wish to register.

Use keywords to target your audience

If you are hoping to gain an audience from those people who utilize search engines, then this will be your first step in optimizing that. You should utilize keywords that you expect people will search when looking for your content. Target those people and the areas who you want to access the content on your site. This way, when they search these terms, or for information in these areas, they can come up with your site.

Avoid numbers and hyphens

Numbers, hyphens, and special characters can make your website confusing and difficult to find. In addition to this, it can make your website confused with those who have the same names without numbers or hyphens. Avoiding these special characters can help your website immensely.

Act Fast

Once you find an available domain name that you like, make sure that you grab it. Domains can be grabbed up quickly and you do not want someone else to steal your idea before it is actually yours.

Buying Your Domain Name

When you get a website through WordPress, you will automatically get a domain name on the WordPress platform. A free WordPress domain name works just fine if you are simply hosting a personal blog, although it does not look very professional.

Instead of your site being displayed as 'http://www.thisismysite.com', it can, by default, only be accessed through 'http://www.thisismysite.wordpress.com'. For business purposes, we don't want that. That's why we will need to register a domain at a domain selling platform. This is a place to buy and register the domain you have chosen for your website. It is important that your domain name of choice is still available, otherwise you cannot claim it for yourself. For the cheapest and easiest solution, I recommend using Namecheap.com to register your domain.

Chapter 4:

Setting Up WordPress

So now it's time to actually get ready setting up WordPress. It's pretty simple, we just need to follow a few basic steps, and have our domain name in place.

Installing WordPress on Your Domain

So you have selected your host, selected your domain name, and downloaded WordPress onto your website from WordPress.org. It is time to install WordPress onto your new domain and link your hosting service. WordPress is well known for being fairly easy to install and use with your website. Most web hosts that you can use offer tools that can help you install WordPress. These tools are available through your hosts website and will be generally easy to use and self-explanatory. However, you are not required to utilize these, you can install WordPress on your own.

The instructions for this can be found at https://codex.wordpress.org/Installing_WordPress. This installation guide gives you a step-by-step guide on using the WordPress easy installation.

Before you install WordPress, make sure that your Web host meets the WordPress minimum requirements, you have downloaded the most current version of WordPress, you unzipped the downloaded file onto your hard drive, and you created a secure password for your WordPress secret key.

What follows is what WordPress describes as the famous five minute install. Do not worry too much if you have issues with this. You can see some of the popular trouble shooting here:
https://codex.wordpress.org/Installing_WordPress.

1. Download and unzip the WordPress package if you haven't already.

2. Create a database for WordPress on your web server, as well as a MySQL (or MariaDB) user who has all privileges for accessing and modifying it.

3. (Optional) Find and rename wp-config-sample.php to wp-config.php, then edit the file (see Editing wp-config.php) and add your database information.

4. Upload the WordPress files to the desired location on your web server:

   - If you want to integrate WordPress into the root of your domain (e.g. http://example.com/), move or upload all contents of the unzipped WordPress directory (excluding the WordPress directory itself) into the root directory of your web server.

   - If you want to have your WordPress installation in its own subdirectory on your website (e.g. http://example.com/blog/), create the blog directory on your server and upload the contents of the unzipped WordPress package to the directory via FTP.

   - ***Note:*** *If your FTP client has an option to convert file names to lower case, make sure it's disabled.*

5. Run the WordPress installation script by accessing the URL in a web browser. This should be the URL where you uploaded the WordPress files.

   - If you installed WordPress in the root directory, you should visit: http://example.com/

   - If you installed WordPress in its own subdirectory called blog, for example, you should visit: http://example.com/blog/.

That's it! WordPress should now be installed.

This may seem complicated and over simplified. If you have more issues installing WordPress, you can check out the detailed instructions and troubleshooting page. WordPress even has instructions for how to install on domains with different host tools like phpMyAdmin, my SQL management, and DirectAdmin. Do not be worried if you have to use these troubleshooting directions. WordPress has a great set-up for help and assistance.

Chapter 5:

About WordPress Themes

Your theme will determine the look and feel of your website. Basically, it is a template that will determine the structure and layout of the content you would be going to deliver on your site.

Choosing your Theme

Choosing your theme is an important part of your website. You want to make sure that the theme you select works well in every way with your website and looks how you want it to. A theme is like a "skin" for your website. Themes change the design, look, and presentation of your website. They can be essential to impressing and working well with those people who visit your site or blog on a regular basis. WordPress themes are able to use template files to change your website's or blog's appearance without changing the underlying software and content.

WordPress is considered an open source website. That means that anyone can upload and share themes and anyone can use them. WordPress believe that there should be many free options available to everyone. WordPress has a theme directory with all of the currently available and tested themes. This theme directory is located at https://wordpress.org/themes/ . Here you can see the popular themes, featured themes, and even search through your own keywords or ideas.

There are many things to consider when you are choosing your WordPress theme. Make sure that you select the right one. You can always change and test out new themes on your WordPress Blog or Website. Make sure that once you select your theme you test it out on your phone, other browsers, and other computers. This way, you can make sure that your new theme for your website or blog works exactly how you want it to work. Here is what you should consider when you are selecting your perfect theme:

- Speed: The speed or your new theme for your website or blog is very important. It is vital that you find one that works for you. Consider how much information and content you will want to be including on each page and what type of audience is viewing each page. Remember to consistently test the speed of your website on multiple platforms.

- Lightweight and Minimalistic: A lightweight or minimalistic theme is going to perform faster than a heavier or flashier theme. These themes have simple patterns and setups. They do not have complex rules and transitions. Lightweight and minimalistic themes do not generally have buttons that do special tricks or strong graphics. If you are going to have content that will take up more speed from the website, this may the best route for you. If you want your website or blog to be simple, quick, and easy to access, a lighter theme may help you provide that.

- OR Heavy and Flashy: A heavy and flashy theme may not be the worst thing possible for your blog either. Sure, the light and minimalistic themes can help provide ease of use and speed. However, the heavier and flashier themes come with more features and exciting tools for your new blog or website. These themes will have more impressive features that may help keep your audience entertained and coming back for more. The content and theme are both very important when doing this.

- User Experience: The number one consideration when selecting a theme is your users experience. You will want to consider what audience you want to attract and how you want that audience to feel about your site and your content. You want to ensure that your audience will have a pleasant experience with your blog or website. This may take some effort and some additional work. You may have to utilize a trial and error method and minor theme adjustments until you find one that works perfectly for you. Even so, the theme may not always work perfectly for you. So don't forget to consistently check on your user experience.

- Ease of Use: Is your theme easy to use? This is another important consideration. If all of your menu options are too close together for your readers to click on and your text is almost unreadable, maybe this theme is not for you. Appearance and speed is important, but ease of use is vital. If someone utilizes your website and has a difficult time, chances are they won't come back. Constantly make sure that your website is easy to use. Test it on your phone, other computers, other networks, and all browsers possible. Different browsers and views can make a theme appear and be used differently. Make sure that your theme makes your blog or site easy to use on every platform possible.

- Mobile Friendliness: Much like the ease of use, the mobile friendliness of your blog or website is vital to keeping consumers around. More than 63% of US adults have smartphones now. That is a huge chunk of the population who is probably looking at your content on a tiny four-inch screen, instead of a larger one. This will not be a problem if you plan your website or blog correctly and make sure that it is very mobile friendly. If it is not mobile friendly, chances are readers will not stay and attempt to read the content, let alone attempt to come back.

- How easy is it to customize? Similarly, the customization is very important. You want to consider how easy it is to make the theme look like you want it to. You do not want your site to look like everyone else's, you want to make it yours. This helps you stand out. Consumers will notice and appreciate the customization. Do not be afraid to scrap a theme just because you do not like the way it customizes. There are thousands more themes for you to choose from. Chances are, something will have what you want.

Premium Themes vs. Free Themes

All of the magical themes available for WordPress are not always free. There are several themes that are premium themes. These premium themes come at a cost. So, the question becomes *Do you spend money on themes, or no?* If you are a beginner, the answer is NO. As you begin to utilize WordPress, find themes that work well for you. Figure out what you need and what you do not need. As time goes on, you will probably want to invest in some premium themes, but at this point you are better off utilizing what you have available for free.

Premium themes do come with their share of advantages that you will want to consider one you get more and more involved and invested into your blog or website. The advantages to the premium themes on WordPress are:

- Better Formatting
- Increased Support
- More Customization
- More Options
- More Unique Ability

It depends on what your goals are. If you are serious about starting a business and your website will be a critical part of your marketing plan (and it should be!), you will probably be better of making a commitment to a paid theme (just make sure it comes from a reputable company and that you test it before purchasing).

If you are unsure of where to start with your theme, I recommend that you take the time to check out the themes GeneratePress and Sparkling. They are both fantastic options for a beautiful web design. Both GeneratePress and Sparkling are completely free and very user friendly.

Customizing Your Theme

When working on your theme, learning and knowing minor HTML will make all of the difference in the world. You can build additional specifications and scripts into your themes. Utilize google to find some good pre-built scripts to aid in the customization of your theme. WordPress has help pages to provide additional support with your theme customization goals.

Testing Your Theme

Make sure that you are consistently testing the looks and performance of the new WordPress theme that you have selected. In addition to this, make sure that you test your theme every time that there is a new WordPress update. Test your theme for usability and performance in all categories. Make adjustments that show all of your content easily and in a way that you want it to be displayed and available.

Chapter 6:

Understanding the WordPress Dashboard

The first step in creating a strong website is to familiarize yourself with the first thing you will see when you log-in. This is the WordPress Dashboard. The dashboard is a necessary part of putting your website together and can be extremely helpful as you continue to expand your website. Here, you can see exactly how your site is doing.

Once you log into your WordPress Admin screen, the first thing you will see if your WordPress Dashboard. Your dashboard is the most necessary and important tool in your WordPress arsenal. The WordPress dashboard gives you the ability to get an at-glance overview of everything that is happening with your blog or website. The dashboard lets you catch up on news, view draft posts, see who is linking to your website, quickly put out posts, or check and moderate comments.

Everything on the dashboard comes in blocks called widgets. There are five defaulted widgets on the dashboard:

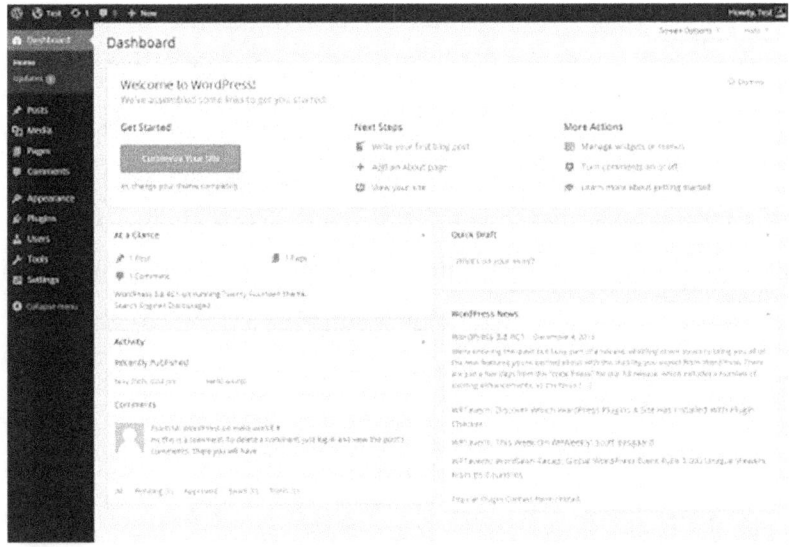

At a glance: At a glance gives you a birds-eye view of everything that is happening with your blog or website. It gives you information like the number of posts, pages, and comments on your website.

Activity: Shows the activity on your blog such and recent comments in need of moderation and scheduled posts.

Quick Draft: This allows you to make a quick no-frills draft for publishing on your website or blog.

WordPress News: This widget keeps you up to date on everything that is happening in the WordPress community.

These widgets can be adjusted, moved, deleted, or added to as time goes on and as you may desire. You can choose which widgets will work best for you as you work on your blog or website. Many plug-in developers make widgets that can be added to your Dashboard. You can also add other widgets to give you quick views on your blog or website. Utilize the "screen options" to choose which widgets you want to see and which ones you do not.

Menu

From the dashboard, the left side of screen you will see the menu to navigate your website. This menu gives you access to everything you need for your website or blog.

Posts

When you are ready to begin adding content to your website or blog, this selection is going to be very helpful to you. Here, you can add pages, add content to any of these pages, edit this content, add media to your posts, and much, much more. Don't forget to tag your posts! This helps get them recognized, get them into search engines, and gives you categories for your posts.

Media

From the media selection, you can add media such as audio files, videos, music, or pictures. Here, there is also a library where you can view and edit all of your previously added media.

Pages

A page is static content. When you add a page, they stay on your website or blog. Typically, you can utilize pages to add "About" sections or "Contact" pages. The All Pages tool helps you edit, add, delete, and organize pages. Utilizing multiple pages is a sign of a well-run, put together website. It helps keep you organized and assists your viewers as they look for specific information.

Comments

Your comments are your reader feedback. This took lets you see and moderate all of the comments that users have posted to any and all of your content. This also gives you access to the Spam comments. Regularly check these comments to make sure that nothing got marked as Spam when it should have been posted. This tool also gives you the ability to set-up or take away moderation and the ability to comment all-together on posts. It is generally better to keep moderation on within your website. This way, inappropriate and Spam comments can be screened out. It may take a little extra work, but it is better than having comments you should not have and having to delete them after the fact. There is a search box that allows you to search for specific comments on your site.

Appearance

Along with "posts," this is one of the most important tools available through your dashboard for your blog or website. Here, you have the power to make your website look the way you want it.

Utilize the theme's tool to change your theme. Remember, that once you select your theme you need to test it very carefully for usability. If you choose to get a premium theme make sure that it comes from a reputable dealer and that you test it before you purchase it.

The customize tool goes along with your theme. Any customizable options that go along with the theme that you select will be displayed and editable here. This is the fun part when you get to change your blog even more to make it the best website possible for everything that you need.

The menus tool gives you the ability to add menus and navigation to present to your website or blog visitors. This is very important when it comes to the usability of your website. If your website is difficult to navigate, those visitors you get may not come back. Make the menus tool a priority for yourself as you continue to work on your website.

The header tool lets you change what is displayed on a theme's header. Make sure you change this, I'm sure you will notice if you don't when you edit the header.

The background feature tool allows you to change the background of your blog.

The theme editor allows you to adjust sections of the coding in your theme. If you have some knowledge of HTML or CSS this tool will assist you even more with your website. This is by no means a required knowledge to have, but as you need your website to do more, it may be a skill worth learning.

Plugins

Plugins are totally awesome and helpful. Plugins are a tool that can be extremely useful for you as you work on your blog or website with WordPress. Your plugins extend and expand the features and functionality of your blog or website. There are nearly fifty-thousand plug-ins currently available to you from WordPress. You can get them from https://wordpress.org/plugins/ where you can search, see the most popular ones, and even see what plug-ins are available for Beta testing.

Installing a plug-in is easy and straightforward. To install a plugin you generally just need to put the plugin file into your 'wp-content/plugins' directory. Once a plugin is installed, you are easily able activate it or deactivate it from the Plugins menu in your WP administration.

On the dashboard, it is easy to add a new plug-in file once you find one that you want to use. From there, you can select which files you want to activate or de-activate.

In WordPress 2.7 and above you can install plugins directly from the admin area. Download the plugin to your computer, then log in to your WP admin area and go to Plugins > Add New.

Browse to the plugin archive and select it. Then click Install Now and the plugin will be installed shortly. The only thing left to do is to navigate to Plugins and click activate for the plugin you just installed on your WordPress website.

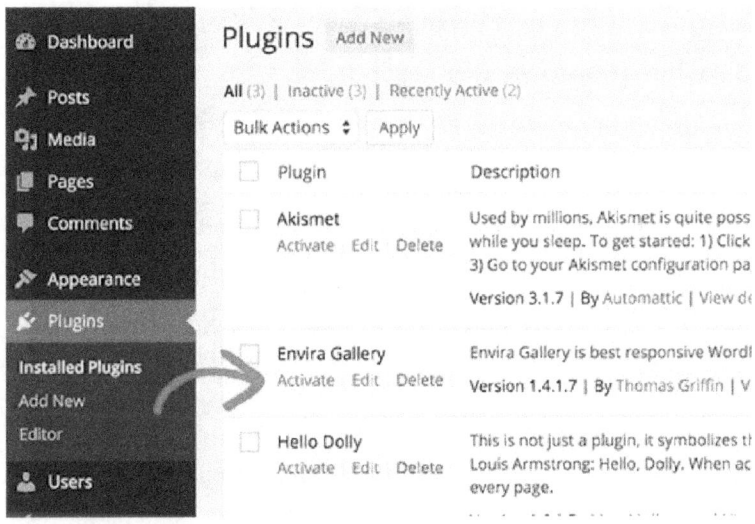

The removal is also straight-forward and easy in most plug-in cases. To remove it, you can simply remove the directory for the plugin you would like to uninstall and it will be automatically deactivated.

Keep in mind that not all plug-ins are easy to install. You can view their specific installation and use when you read them on the WordPress.org website.

Users

Each blog or website has at least one user, but you can add more. Many people have others involved in their blog or website who they want to be able to add content on their own. If you want another person to be able to post to your blog or generate content on your website, that person must have access to a user account; typically, every person will have her or his own user account.

That is what this users tab is for on the dashboard, from the Users option in the main navigation menu you have the ability to set up all of the user accounts you need. You can also change a user's information or even delete them. This can make managing your blog or website much easier.

Do not forget to take advantage of the important administrative feature here is the Roles feature. Depending on their Role, different users have different capabilities.

Tools

The tools app, located on the main navigation menu, is intended to be very helpful to you and your blog or website. Here, you are given the ability to speed up WordPress for your local machine, import content from other sources, export your content, or to upgrade your WordPress software to a new release. Keep this in mind, because keeping your software updated is very important.

Chapter 7:

Essential Plugins

Plugins are definitely very important in your search to have the best blog or website out there. Your plugins extend and expand the features and functionality of your blog or website. There are nearly fifty-thousand plug-ins currently available to you from WordPress. You can get them from https://wordpress.org/plugins/ where you can search, see the most popular ones, and even see what plug-ins are available for Beta testing.

Visit the previous chapter if you are having trouble installing plug-ins on your website. This can be tricky if you try to do so without any help or assistance. Do not be afraid to look it up and take advantage of this book or the resources online through WordPress.

There are a nearly endless supplies of plugins available to you as you put together your website or blog. There are over forty-five thousand plugins and they have been downloaded over a million times.

Plugins are essential to running your blog or website and having the best experience for your users. It can help you customize your blog to do everything you need it to. Here are a few different categories that are essential to running your blog or website. In each category, there will be an explanation of what you want your plugins to do and what plugins are available now that other people have found helpful.

SEO (Search Engine Optimization)

Search engine optimization is crucial to running your blog or website. If you want people to hit your site based on web searches, you want to work with search engine optimization. SEO plugins allow webmasters to easily optimize certain elements of a website's code and structure to make it more noticeable and workable by search engine spiders. Just having the SEO plugin alone won't improve your company's search engine rankings. You still need to write a title tag and Meta description that's optimized for the keywords your customers are using to search online for products and services. If you utilize a good SEO plugin and put the effort it, you will see positive results through your blog or website. Invest time in your SEO and you will see positive results. Here are a few of the top performing SEO plugins around today:

- <u>All in One SEO Pack</u> – This plugin is very popular on WordPress. It is one of the top performing overall plugins available on WordPress. The All in One SEO Pack gives you some great tools to help optimize SEO for your blog or website. Some of the benefits that this plugin totes include: google analytics support, Automatically notifies search engines like Google and Bing about changes to your site, ONLY free plugin to provide SEO Integration for e-Commerce sites, including WooCommerce, Generates META tags automatically, compatible with many other plugins, and translated into 57 other languages. The All in

One SEO Pack is regularly updated and has many good reviews.

- Yoast SEO – Yoast SEO is a great way to keep yourself focused and up-to-date. Yoast also boasts a lot of different tools to help you improve content. It is regularly updated as well. It first and foremost helps you write better content. Yoast SEO forces you to choose a focus keyword when you're writing your articles, and then makes sure you use that focus keyword everywhere.

Analytics

Learning more about your users is vital to running a successful online business website or blog. You need an analytics solution that helps you gather data and provide insightful reports into user activity on your site. Without this tool, you cannot know who is visiting your site and why. Having stronger analytics helps you create content that is going to work well with your audience and keep those readers and users coming back time and time again. A good analytics platform can tell you where your users are coming from, which pages they are visiting the most, how long do they stay on your website. You want to know which links they are clicking on and much more. This is all where the analytics plugins come into play. Here are a few good analytics plugins you can utilize to help with this portion of running your website or blog. Make sure that you take advantage of them and utilize them in a way that helps your business. It is not enough to simply download the correct plugin, you must also utilize it and take it into consideration.

- Google Analytics – Google analytics in the most popular analytics tool available, even though it is not necessarily a plugin. It is free, and very easy to install.

- Google Analytics Plugin for WordPress - The Google Analytics for WordPress allows you to track your blog easily and always stays up to date with the newest features in Google Analytics. This plugin uses the universal or the asynchronous Google Analytics tracking code, the fastest and most reliable tracking code Google Analytics offers. Gives you incredibly nice visitor metric dashboards right in your WordPress install. Option to enable demographics and interest reports. This plugin utilized google analytics to an even more positive degree.

Website Speed

Website speed certainly matters. No matter if it is driven over a WordPress script or on any other, you need to consider the average page load time consistently with your website or blog. There is no particular line over here, which should be considered the best but you need to look over making the website work as fast as it can. WordPress is pretty impressive. The large amount of plugins can be utilized to your advantage as you work with the speed of your website and try to improve it. Here are some plugins that you can utilize to increase the speed of your website. Remember that increasing the speed of your website can increase the popularity and the chances of your users and readers coming back time and time again. Here are some suggested speed increasing plugins.

- WP-Optimize – You may not even realize it, but every time you hit 'Update' on a post you are slowing down your WordPress site. Every time you save a post or a page, WordPress creates a revision and stores it on your MySQL overhead. If you work in your WordPress editor, you are most likely constantly saving. Having this many revisions, drafts, and items can choke off your WordPress site speed if you are not careful. This plugin is intentionally made to help with this issue.

- WP Super Cache – When a reader visits your site, their browser has to load a ton of items including logos, the CSS file, and the resources associated with your blog. This is why websites take time to load, and some of them take a lot of time to load. Using browser caching, your browser remembers the items it had to load on the first page it accessed so it doesn't have to load them up again. The WP Super Cache plugin helps with this by generating a static html file from your WordPress blog. Once the html file is created, your server uses that instead of processing the much bigger PHP scripts to users. The plugin runs automatically once it's uploaded and enabled. Thankfully, this is one that you should be able to load and forget about. However, do not forget to update it and work out the advanced settings if you need it.

Setting up a Shop

You might find that you want to sell products through your WordPress website. This is totally awesome! Do not be discouraged about all of the different features, many users have done this already, and so there are many plugins available for you to use to set up a shop and sell your products.

- WooCommerce – Woocommerce is one of the most popular plugins for shop owners and those who want to utilize WordPress to sell items. This had lots of top-of-the-line features; it is powerful and highly extendable. One of the best things about WooCommerce is that it has a large collection of free and paid themes and extensions. Key features of WooCommerce include PayPal Standard integration, sales and reviews reports, multiple shipping options, flexible couponing system and easy inventory management.

- Easy Digital Downloads – Digital downloads can be tough to sell, but they can be great fun and very profitable. Easy Digital Downloads is solely intended for selling digital downloads via WordPress at no cost. Rather than including a lot of useless features like other plug-ins, Easy Digital Downloads has kept selling digital goods simple and streamlined by providing only most useful features. It also includes a powerful reporting system that allows you to see all of your earnings and sales through graphs and easy to analyze data tables.

- Simple PayPal Shopping Cart – This simple solution to ecommerce through your WordPress site allows you to add a PayPal checkout shopping cart to your website. This plugin lets you add an 'Add to Cart' button to any product on any pages or posts. It lets you display the cart simply. You can add the cart to sidebars or display it on any page.

From this, anyone can check out after viewing their items.

Make sure you regularly clean up plugins that are on your blog or website. You do not want to keep plugins around that you are not using. They can slow down your blog and be a hassle later on. In addition to this, regularly make sure that all of your plugins are working and doing what you want them to do.

Check the reviews on a plugin before you install it on a website. Do not just assume that it will work and do what you want it to do.

Just like how you would not buy a product on Amazon without checking the review, you need to check the reviews on a plugin before you install it. By doing this, you will save yourself the time it takes to uninstall a plugin and find a new one that does what you want. Your time is valuable as you run a website or blog. Take the time to do it right.

Chapter 8:

Adding Content to Your WordPress Site

Adding Content to Your WordPress Website or Blog (Adding Posts)

Content is perhaps one of the most important parts of your website or blog. Even if you have the best design in the world, you will not really have visitors (let alone repeat visitors) if you do not have content on your blog or website. Adding content to your WordPress website or blog is not something you want to do without fully understanding it; make sure you add content in the correct and best way as often as possible. Content is an important aspect of search engine optimization, it is part of how Search Engines like Google, Yahoo, and Bing determine where to rank your website. The content is entirely up to you, write whatever you want, just make sure you share it with the world to help working on your website or blog.

In WordPress, you can either write posts or Pages to keep your readers interested and excited. When you are writing a regular blog entry, you write a post. Posts, in a default setup, will appear in reverse chronological order on your blog's home page. Pages are for content such as "About," "Contact," etc. Pages exist away from the normal blog chronology. Pages are often used to present timeless information (that does not expire and that you want your readers and users to be able to consistently easily access) about yourself or your site. You can even use Pages to organize and manage any content.

However, if you just want to keep adding items to your blog or website, if you want to add updated content ready to view, you will want to use the "posts" function.

Here are the steps you must follow to add a post to your online blog or website through WordPress:

1. Log in to your WordPress Dashboard
2. Click on the 'Posts' tab
3. Click on the 'Add New' sub tab

4. Fill in the blanks on the page that appears: Enter your title, enter your main body, and adjust the post as necessary.

5. Make sure that you are knowledgably adding categories, tags, and editing settings for your post.

6. When you are ready and finished you select 'publish.' If you are not ready yet or you do not want it to be published just yet, you can save your post as a draft and even schedule it to post at a later date.

Here are some of the important considerations you should have when you add content to your blog or website:

- Use Paragraphs - No one likes to read writing that never pauses for a break or is laid out in one big chunk. This is a really quick way to lose readers based on your content. You can break your writing up into paragraphs: just use double spaces between your paragraphs and WordPress will automatically detect these and insert <p> HTML paragraph tags into your writing. This is a simple step that many bloggers can miss, it can be devastating to your blog. Do not forget your paragraphs.

- Use Headings - If you are writing long posts, do not forget to break up the sections by using headings. Headings are small titles to highlight a change of subject much like the bolded parts of this chapter.

In HTML, headings are set by the use of h1, h2, h3, h4, and so on. By default, most WordPress Themes use the first, second, and sometimes third heading levels within the site. You can use h4 to set your own headings. If this all seems too confusing, do not hesitate to visit https://codex.wordpress.org/Designing_Headings to learn more about designing and using headings.

- Spell Check and Proofread – Readers do not want to read information from someone who they feel cannot write. There are tools on the WordPress editing page to spell check and proof your post. You do not need to rely upon these, there are a million different tools available online everywhere from grammerly.com (where you can have your posts proofed by an automatic tool) to the online Khan Academy where you can take free courses on writing, grammar, spelling, and punctuation.

- Write and Post Often – Readers prefer to see consistent content. Create a writing schedule and stick to it. A blog without consistent content has very little value.

- Utilize Pictures, Videos, Media, and Even Menus – The next sections of this chapter will tell you more about doing these for your blog. All of these areas can improve the experience that your visitors will have, which can only positively benefit you and your website or blog.

Adding Pictures

Adding pictures to your posts or pages can totally change and upgrade the dynamic of your blog or website. These are fantastic tools to utilize as you create content and hope to bring in more readers. Make sure that you have good, quality images for your posts. It is very simple to add images to your posts.

1. Place your curser where you want the picture: In order to add a picture to your page or post, you must first insert your cursor text where you want the picture to be at. If you want images in line with the text, you can place your curser within your text. If you want the image to appear by itself, simply place your curser on a blank line.

2. Click the Add Media Button

3. Add or Select the Image that You Want to Use: You have two options here. If you have already uploaded the picture that you want you can select it from the media library. However, if you have not, select 'upload files.' From here you can upload the picture or pictures that you want and they will be added to your media library where you can select them.

4. Determine Your Attachment Details: Once you select your image, the 'Attachment Details' pane

will appear. This shows a small un-cropped thumbnail of the image, as well as important information such as the filename, date uploaded, and image dimensions in pixels. Here, there are action links that allow you to edit the image (which will take you to the 'Edit Image' page) or to delete the image permanently from your site if you happen to choose the wrong one or decide you do not want to use it anymore. In addition to this, you can edit the following media information on your image: Title, Caption (This text is displayed below the image), Alternate Text, and Description of the image.

Embedding Videos

It is very easy to embed videos into your WordPress site or blog. Doing so can add an extra level of pleasantry to your blog or website. Make sure that the URL is not a hyperlink and is its own line. On YouTube you can click the 'embed' link on most videos and get the perfect link for your WordPress site or Blog.

Now, all you have to do is insert the link into the text of the post where you would like to see it embedded. WordPress is totally awesome and will automatically detect that it is there and embed the video into the blog for you. Now, your readers can view the video without having to leave your blog.

Be careful! Do not add too many videos without reason. This will make your website slower and the loading will be difficult. Make sure to consistently check your blog for speed and ensure that the videos are not slowing it down unnecessarily.

Adding other Media

If you want to add any other media, it can be done one of two ways. You can follow the steps of adding an image into your post and instead upload another form of media, or you can embed it much like you would embed a video, just copy the link.

Just like with the videos, having too much media can slow down your website, so make sure you use this sparingly. Do not have ten videos trying to automatically play on your home screen, this is a quick way to lose readers before they get anywhere near the rest of your content.

Chapter 9:

Tips for a Successful WordPress Site

Test, test and test: Test your website, then test it again. Test every single link of your website or blog on every single browser. Test your website on your phone. Test it on another operating system. Then, test it on a tablet. Ask your friends to test and comment on your website. You can even pay someone to test your website for you. There are several where sites you can get your website tested and commented on by various real people in real time. Some of these websites, like fiverrr.com, will help you find someone to test your website for as little as $5.

Publish Regularly: Make sure that you are keeping your blog or website up to date. This does not mean that you should stick to a schedule of posting, but you should plan out your posting and content carefully. Make sure that you are paying attention to what your audience is responding to and publishing that sort of content. Do not be over-ambitious. Make sure that you do what you are capable of, but are still publishing regularly. Set a publishing schedule, identify new ideas and plan them in advance, draft new posts, edit those posts well, and regularly share those posts in a manner that attracts readers to them. If you are utilizing search engine optimization software, make sure that you plan out your keywords and organize your posts in a positive manner. Utilize the plug-ins talked about in the previous chapter to help you out with all of this.

High Quality Content: Your users and readers do not want to see the same stock-image on every single site that they visit. They want good content, good pictures, and quality videos. If you are building an online shopping experience make sure that you provide high quality pictures with views from every angle and strong explanations. Do not just simply provide one picture and assume that is enough. Consumers will not purchase what they do not understand or know well. One way to make sure that they understand and know well is to create high quality content and utilize quality images to showcase your items. Both items that you are trying to sell and content posts/articles are able to impact your audience more if they have high quality media associated with them.

SEO Optimization: One of the most important and useful ways you can increase traffic to your website is through search engines. Even if you feel as though you are consistently at the top of your market and working better than any of your competitors, do not skimp on search engine optimization. You will easily lose all of your market value if you do this to yourself. Utilize plug-ins and do constant research on what you emphasize and how you can improve your search engine optimization skills. Cater your content: optimize your names, titles, descriptions, and content for search engines and performance. You will not regret putting in this extra work. Just like you should schedule blog posts and set-ups, you should schedule time to work on search engine optimization.

- **Consistently Consider All Options:** Stay on top of looking for new platforms, plugins, helpful tools, hints, and additions all the time. Amazing and awesome products are being released every day, and there might be the very ones you needed, but never knew existed. If you stay on top of new and old options, eventually you may find what you need. Do not become complacent in your blog. In fact, you can always make a list of crucial solutions, and utilize at least three of them for a closer look. It does not mean that you have to use the popular plugins and consistently follow trends. However, instead it means that you will find a thing or two that can make your WordPress blog or website better, and if you blog or website is better, than you will be better, you will create better content, and you will attract more readers, users, and customers.

- **Promote, promote, and promote some more:** Social media is one of today's greatest powers. It can provide you with great opportunities to share your work with the world. Facebook has over three million users and mobile social media gains over one million users per day. This can be an important thing to forget. Find family and friends to help you out. Share. Use buzz words. Social media can be difficult to manage, but if you stay on top of it and utilize it right, it will help you, your business, and your website immensely. Social media can be one of the most helpful tools for your store, blog, or website because you can share your products, articles and blogs there, and interact with customers, readers, and users among your target audience. The best way to start is to attach social sharing icons on the product pages, content, blog posts, and everything else on your site. You can even reward viewers that are sharing your content on a specific network, which is one of the best ways to be more exposed in front of social media followers.

- **Speed up Your Site:** A single, solitary second of loading time on your website can have a 7% reaction. The longer the load, the less likely the customer is to come back, let alone see what you have to offer. In today's fast paced world, no one wants to wait on you. Do not make them if you want your readers to return. Speed is vital for success. Make sure you have the right hosting, do not add too much video content or too many advertisements, keep your pop-ups to a minimum, and take advantage of speed boosting plugins.

- **Update Regularly:** Update your website or blog regularly, especially when you're using WordPress plugins. Any useful plugin is going to have consistent updates to continue to help you. Having extra plugins can even slow your blog or website down and cost you much needed traffic. Take good care of the products you are downloading and utilizing. Some of them can even compromise your website's security policy. One of the most difficult parts of running a WordPress website or blog is that better and improved versions of WordPress itself, tools, and plugins are appearing day by day, and you have to keep an eye on them in order to improve the user experience and keep your readers coming back daily and appreciating your content. Unedited and irresponsive plugins are the easiest way for hackers to attack your website, simply by staying on track with developments you can keep both intruders and bugs out of your way. Make sure you are doing this at least to protect yourself and your customers.

- **Do Not Forget About Mobile Friendliness:** WordPress websites, blogs, and stores have no choice but to be mobile-friendly if they want to grow in this market, and there is no compromising on it! Phones and tablets have become the principal devices people use to do online shopping, reading, and learning. If your website or blog is not accessible and easy to ready from a mobile phone, you will undoubtedly lose visitors. If your site or blog is difficult to use or read from a phone, your readers and users will go somewhere else for the content they desire. Mobile sites for blogs and websites can fall behind the technology curve in a matter of months, and more likely, a matter of weeks. Keep on top of your mobile friendliness so you do not unknowingly miss out on customers. Some of the diagnostics and analytics plugins you can utilize on a regular basis can even tell you how many mobile readers and users you are getting. Paying attention to this will help you determine what kind of mobile advances you need and how much attention to need to be paying to your mobile site.

Chapter 10: Parting Words

Building an awesome website is a process. A tool such as WordPress only simplifies the building of that place a little more. As with all tools, it takes time to understand and learn, and will not always cooperate the way you wish it would. This guide will certainly be a helpful *tool* in the process of getting to know the online world a little bit better.

I hope this short guidebook has given you some more in-depth insight into the topic, and will lead you on a path towards a successful WordPress project. One that will not be without obstacles, but certainly a path that will be worthwhile.

Hopefully you are now a little bit more knowledgeable on the topic and will be able to start focusing on the project your website will be about, instead of all the technicalities surrounding it. A journey into the online business world is always an interesting opportunity to discover more about marketing and business, and possibly making a lot of money in the process. Blogging is even one of the coolest ways to make money online! All the best in your life, and my gratitude for giving me the opportunity to get you on your way with your project.

SEO

Step By Step Beginners Guide to Search Engine Optimization For Web Traffic Growth

Book 2

Arnold De Vries

Table of Contents

Chapter 1: Introduction

So you want more people to come to your website... Big surprise, so do literally all the other websites on the internet! But you know something about 95% of website owners don't have a single clue about: the importance of Google rankings and optimization for those rankings.

And by reading this step-by-step introduction into Search Engine Optimization (SEO), you will have gained a competitive edge that will potentially make you thousands of dollars on the internet.

So pat yourself on the back, because you made a great decision. You just took your first baby steps into the magic world that is SEO: a world where you have the ability to tame the mighty beast that is Google. The Big G is known to change its algorithm recipe a lot though, so it's a good idea to get the basics down and keep learning as much as possible in your journey.

Utilizing this book to help you make sure you are ready to take on your search rankings adventure. You will learn from the beginning what steps you need to take to influence and improve your website for Google. No prior knowledge required. If you do have some knowledge already, then great, you have a head start!

This in-depth guide will help you navigate through the jungle of Anchor text strategies, keyword research, setting up a private blog network and many other useful features to optimize your site. So, starting from nothing, let's get that website going. The following chapters will help you get started with ease.

Chapter 2: The Basics of SEO

In order for visitors to find your website, it is evident that you work with Google's optimization guidelines. In the world of Search Engine Optimization (SEO), there's however much more to be discovered.

Let's start by breaking down the absolute basics of SEO. This chapter will go onto what exactly SEO is, why you need it, and will give an overview of relevant terms that are used in the SEO space.

What is SEO?

Search Engine Optimization (in short: SEO) is, above all, a way to generate traffic to your website. Many people focusing on SEO as an internet marketing strategy seem to forget about this. It is one of many ways to attract targeted traffic to the place you want them the most: your corner of the World Wide Web.

Three major distinctions exist, and depending on the type of website you are building, your path will be greatly determined by these major categories of SEO:

1. **Global SEO:** Often used in congruency with content marketing – ranking your site for broad keywords that are relevant to your site. Global SEO is the opposite of Local SEO.

2. **Affiliate SEO:** Generating traffic for certain product promotions is one of the most lucrative ways to earn money with SEO. Affiliate marketing is a great monetization strategy for your website – This could be product promotion, lead generation or even generating phone calls for clients.

3. **Local SEO:** The act of ranking for geo-sensitive search terms. Or in plain English: physical

locations become your keywords. For example, if you have a bakery in downtown Manhattan, you attempt to rank your website about your business for search terms such as: "Manhattan bakery", "New York bread shop", or "NYC Manhattan wholegrain".

Glossary

In the world of SEO's, there's a lot of fancy words floating around. These might confuse beginners, so let's list a few of the most widely used. This is by no means an exhaustive list of terms, but it's helpful to refer to when you're confused what a certain term means:

301 Redirect: A 301 server redirect is the change of a webpage to another page on that same domain (usually the homepage). Used in expired domains to keep the link juice of no longer existing pages.

Adwords: Google service for paid webpage clicks. Essentially used for advertisements on Google for any given search term. The Adwords Keyword Planner tool is a very useful tool for easy and free keyword research.

Algorithm: The lines of code used by programmers to shape the search rankings. We do know the broad outlines of the Google search algorithm, but we can never know it precisely (the only people who know work at Google).

Alt Text: Google's algorithm cannot read images very well. We give alt text keywords to an image in order to let google know the relevance of the contents of the image. Essentially, this is the invisible title for an image only Google can see.

Anchor Text: The exact match text that links to your website. Is explained in detail in a later chapter of this book.

Authority: How powerful Google deems your website or page to be. Often measured using Majestic / Ahrefs / Moz metrics.

Backlinks: The links you are receiving from external websites, which point to a certain page within your own website

Black Hat SEO: The so-called 'dark side' of SEO practices that is not necessarily within the Google Terms of Use. Use at own risk, although often highly effective.

Bounce Rate: How quickly people tend to leave your site. Essentially this is the percentage of visitors on your site that only visit one page and leave very quickly again.

Breadcrumbs: Will show the exact path a visitor of a website has taken. Beneficial to on-page SEO.

Canonical issues: Issues with duplicate content. This means you have multiple webpages on your site with the exact same content – horrible for SEO purposes because Google punishes this hard.

CMS: Content Management System. Basically the software that is used to build a website. The most commonly applied CMS by SEO's is WordPress.

Citation Flow (CF): Majestic SEO metric that indicated the amount of links coming in to a certainly website. Less important than Trust Flow (TF). Optimally you want this to have a >15 value.

Crawler: A bot that quickly analyses all pages on a website.

Duplicate Content: See canonical issues.

Google Dance: The shift in Google ranking positions (See SERP) that is the result of the algorithm used by Google. Usually happens when using PBN sites (which will be explained in a later chapter in this book).

Inbound Links: Links from other websites coming into your website. This is generally regarded as a good thing, especially when the domain that refers to your site has a high authority in Google's eyes.

Indexing / Getting indexed: Google automatically will allow your site to show up in their search engine. This means your page or site is indexed.

Keyword Density: How often the keyword(s) you are targeting are present on a page. Not spamming the keyword is recommended. A few times mentioned is good (especially if it's in the H1-title tags of your article).

Keyword Research: The act of looking for certain words of phrases people are actively looking for on Google. Related to the topic of the website.

Keyword Stuffing: The act of putting as much keywords in your 'Google blurb' (the little text that you see if you search on Google) as possible without making it look unnatural.

Link Building: The act of gathering links to your personal website

Link Exchange: To avoid at all costs. A scheme in which links are exchanged between websites. Often used by directory websites where you have to include a link to the directory in exchange for a link to your site. This will have zero impact on your rankings.

Link Farm: Group of sites all linking to each other. Bad SEO.

Link Juice: The good stuff. If a link is created between website A and B. The power or 'juice' is passed on to that page.

Link Text: See Anchor Text

Long Tail: Keywords which have multiple words attached to them. Very specific search terms.

Meta Tag: HTML in the Head section of a page that gathers certain information. Not visible on the page itself. Is visible to Google's Crawl Engine.

NoFollow Links: These links are ignored by Google for ranking purposes. They occur naturally on all websites and are important to add into the mix of inbound links.

NoIndex Links: Page not indexed at all by Google Crawler. Page will thus never show up in Google at all when a No Index HTML is inserted into the Head of the page's HTML.

Non Reciprocal Link: These types of links have the most value. Basically, if Site B links to your site (Site A), and you do NOT link back to site B, it's a non-reciprocal link.

Organic Link: Not created by SEO, but gained by someone who found your site important or relevant enough to include on their website. Happy days.

Redirect: Certain URL that immediately points to another URL. Will carry over link juice.

Scraping: Using a bot to find expired domains which have high power metrics.

Trust Flow (TF): Majestic SEO metric indicating the power links coming in to a certain domain. More important than Citation Flow (CF). Optimally you want this to have a >13 value.

SERP: Search Engine Results Page. Refers to the position of your page in the Google results page.

Social Bookmarking: Social Media form in which bookmarks are aggregated for public access.

Web 2.0: Websites that encourage user interaction. Examples are Tumblr Blogs, WordPress blogs, etc.

White Hat SEO: The type of SEO that adhere to Google's best practices guidelines. Difficult to pull off compared to black hat SEO. Examples include guest posting, using press releases, or good old-fashioned 'asking another website owner for a link'-method.

Widget: Applications used on webpages for easier use. Often used in WordPress sites.

Why Is SEO Important?

SEO is a way to generate traffic to your website, so the importance simply lies in the fact that 'doing SEO' will give you more people to your site. And if you monetize your website in a clever way, you will indeed be able to get very wealthy from it.

Whilst there are multiple ways to generate traffic to your website, SEO is so lucrative simply because you can decide which terms to rank for. And consequently, how targeted this traffic will be. Finding the perfect terms to rank highly for in Google will absolutely help your online business to grow and flourish.

Should I Only Do SEO?

No. You should not only 'do SEO'. Even the most hardcore evangelists of the SEO world will diversify their traffic generation strategies at some point in time. Only doing SEO is literally throwing your site at the mercy of Google's algorithm. I always advice people to use SEO as a main way to lead organic traffic to their website, but also explore other options. If Google changes their rules on how to rank websites (which they did on multiple occasions in their history), you might potentially lose ALL your website traffic. So it's great advice to also be very active on social media (which in turn will automatically boost your website's SEO rankings, by the way). There's a multitude of other options to explore in order to generate traffic to your website:

- Social media interactions
- Google AdWords
- Facebook advertising
- Offline marketing campaigns
- Network marketing

And this is by no means an exhaustive list of traffic generation options. Traffic generation is an endless fount of resources and possibilities. You will often even see that different traffic generation methods are complementary to each other. However, SEO is certainly one of the most effective ways, if you know what you are doing. Let's dive into the details.

Chapter 3: Keyword Research

Before you even start considering building your website, you should perform a general search of relevant keywords in your particular niche or target market. Following the famous 80/20-principle (where 80% of the results come from 20% of the effort put into something), the act of keyword research is the 20% for achieving SEO results.

Many different methods exist of performing proper keyword research, but I'll explain a very basic and easy (and free) way of finding relevant keywords to target. The tool we will be using for this is called the Google Keyword Planner.

Google Keyword Planner

What better place to check if a keywords gets monthly searches than using Google's data itself? That's why the free to use tool Google Keyword Planner is perfect for keyword research. Admittedly, using the tool is somewhat of a pain sometimes, but at least it's a great free alternative to tools like Long Tail Pro (which have a monthly fee).

The Keyword Planner is actually part of Google AdWords, which is the tool you can use to create paid advertisements on Google's search engine for specific keywords.

Finding the Keyword planner can be complicated because you need a Gmail account to be able to use it, and go through a little maze to find it. Here's the steps:

- Type in 'Google Keyword Planner' in Google
- Click top result
- Log in with your email data
- Register if needed (only once)
- Navigate using the top menu to 'Helpful Tools'
- Click on the keyword planner
- Set your targeting range to your preferred nation you wish to target with your website
- Add your keywords that are somewhat related to your niche in the 'Your Product or Service' box at the top.

The results should look something like the image below. You can choose from Ad group ideas, which are clusters of keywords related to what you entered in your keyword box, or you can look for specific keywords using the tab called 'keyword ideas'. Average monthly searches might no longer be very specific, these have been switched with an estimation.

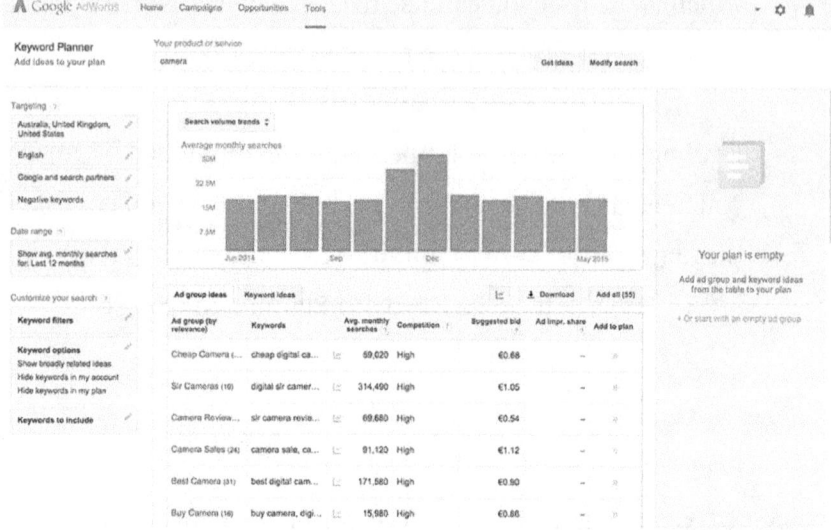

What Google Keyword Planner should look like

Logic dictates that you wish to select high search volumes with low competition. However, you may also want to go for low volume search keywords with high competition, if there's a buyer intent behind a certain keyword (such as 'product X review' or 'best product X 2017'.

Understanding Keywords

There's a real science behind choosing and understand what keywords to choose for SEO targeting. Whilst most of this will come from simply doing and having experience with what works and what doesn't, here's a few beginner's directions. By following the tips below you will be able to better understand which keywords to choose.

Know your niche

What problem are people trying to solve when they look for your website? What products do these people want to buy or what information would they like to know? Understand the needs of your target audience. Once you have a clear view of what your audience would like to know or have, that's when you can start looking for keywords related to that.

Go for long-tail

It's pretty normal that the search terms you're trying to show up for have a lot of competition. That's why it's a good strategy to adapt your keyword research and go for longer phrases people are typing into the Google search bar. These types of keywords are referred to as 'long-tail keywords'. And of course, these words need to be specific to your website topic.

Check competitiveness

This goes back to the previous point: don't try to rank for keywords with high competition. Focus on the low competition ones, preferably those with a lot of people that are looking for those keywords. If you have barely any competition, it will be much easier for your new website to show up high in the Google search rankings.

Make a clear overview

When you do keyword research, open up an Excel sheet (or similar) and write down ALL keywords you have found in a list. Mark the most important ones and also write down the competition level, search volume and some additional thoughts about the keywords you found (for example which category they belong to). A clear mind and good research starts with good documentation. Having an overview of your keywords does that for you.

Know What Your Competition Does

A simple strategy I like to use is to actually go out and see what other websites are doing. Obviously, I will only look at the websites that are ranked at the top for the keyword I'd like to be number 1 at with my own website.

There are numerous tools that will allow you to identify the keyword strategies for certain websites, but in my experience the one that has worked best is called SemRush (it's an expensive SEO tool). So if you're serious about this SEO thing I highly recommend you to take a quick peek at what they allow you to do.

You could also just get a quick website analysis by looking at the Sitemap of a competing site, or run Xenu Link Sleuth (a free software tool) to see what links and pages a competing site has got going on. The idea is to 'borrow' the keywords your competitors are using, because these have obviously worked very well to get their site to the top of Google.

Now that you've got an idea of what keywords to target for your new site, it's time to put it into action. We will implement our keywords on our site using what is known as 'on-page SEO'. The details are found in the next chapter.

Chapter 4: On-Page SEO

Now we know what keywords to target, it's time to break down the act of 'doing SEO' on your site. It's not really complicated at all, but you need to know what components to address. In general, SEO is made up out of the following three elements:

- **On-Page SEO:** Using site-relevant keywords in your website pages, so Google can determine the relevance of your site for certain search terms. Determined by (in diminishing importance): page or post titles, URL description keywords, outbound links, links from one page in your website to another, image alt texts, embedded videos, H1-title tags, and relevant content text keywords.

- **Off-Page SEO:** Gathering relevant backlinks to your website, preferably with good anchor text diversification. This means that the links that point to your website have been placed with relevant keywords in them, but not in a manner that makes them look spammy in any way. More about link building and off-page SEO can be found in the next chapter.

- **Social SEO:** This element of SEO is becoming more and more important recently. Having consistent social media activity supports your on- and off-page SEO and will be the secret sauce on top of your ranking efforts. Social SEO means to place links to your site or articles from social media accounts with high power to them. These could be Web 2.0's, or similar.

Optimizing Your Website

The optimization of a website is performed using good on-site SEO. Generally, people who do SEO will be building their site using WordPress, which allows them to install SEO plugins in order to track the on-site SEO performance.

Recommended plugins to track SEO are called 'All-in-One SEO Pack' and 'Yoast SEO'. Both work equally well, but have different systems to them. It's a matter of preference. If you wish to learn more about WordPress and SEO, please consider reading my other book on WordPress website creation. A link to this WordPress book can be found in the final chapter of this book. I highly recommend checking it out, so you will be quickly on your way to get the best performing SEO website.

Forging A Perfect SEO-Optimized Page

Quick disclaimer: I do not promise you this will work for you. I do not promise you this will even work tomorrow. But this is what has worked for me, and what works right now as I write this book. I'm positive at least some of this will continue to be relevant forever, so hopefully this will help in your own SEO optimization process.

Let's try to forge the perfect storm for a basic page on your website. What can you do to optimize it so Google will love it? Let's look at the on-page SEO factors in diminishing relevance. We will take the example of a bakery website that's trying to rank high in Google for the keyword 'Chocolate Donuts'. On the next page you can find what such a page COULD look like. The layout, however, does not matter one single bit for SEO purposes. So do not be afraid to diversify.

The "Perfectly" Optimized Page

(for the example keyword phrase "chocolate donuts")

Page Title: Chocolate Donuts | Mary's Bakery

Meta Description: Mary's Bakery's chocolate donuts are possibly the most delicious, perfectly formed, flawlessly chocolately donuts ever made.

H1 Headline:
Chocolate Donuts from Mary's Bakery

Image Filename:
chocolate-donuts.jpg

Photo of Donuts
(with Alt Attribute):
Chocolate Donuts

Body Text:_____
_____chocolate donuts_____
_____
_____donuts_____
_____
_____
_____
_____chocolate donuts__
_____

_____
_____donuts_____
_____
chocolate_____
_____
_____
_____
_____chocolate donuts_____
_____
_____chocolate_____
_____
_____
_____
_____
_____chocolate donuts_____
_____

Page URL: http://marysbakery.com/chocolate-donuts

Page title (H1 Headline)

Obviously, your page title should have your exact keyword in it, preferably the very first word(s). Keep the title as short as possible, no keyword stuffing. Also place your exact match keyword title in your Meta Description Title (which happens automatically sometimes). This is the little blurb that you see showing up when you search for websites in Google.

Page URL keyword

In the example, we target chocolate donuts. But our website is called www.marysbakery.com. Make sure that your URL is as short as humanly possible. You can adapt this in the website setting if you're working in WordPress. For our example site, the most ideal situation for SEO purposes is making our page URL: http://marysbakery.com/chocolate-donuts. And nothing more. Then it's perfect if you are targeting chocolate donuts. The key is to place your exact match keyword directly behind your domain URL. And no other symbols, letters, numbers, or unneeded nonsense. Keep it clean.

Meta description

This is one of the most important on-page SEO elements that is technically 'off-page'. Because the Meta description for a page will not show up on your website, but on Google. The description is nothing more than the little blurb of text you see under a page link, when you search for something in Google. The trick is to place our example keyword 'chocolate donuts' at the front of the Meta description title, but also at least once somewhere in the description text. I highly recommend to also include a synonym or similar word to your keyword in your description text, because Google's algorithm will pick up on this. Don't just dump or stuff keywords, but make it a coherent piece of text that someone is eager to click. It's like a tiny sales letter for your page, on Google.

Outbound link to authority site

This is omitted from the example image above, but extremely important for SEO. Add an outbound link to an authority website (a website that is deemed super powerful) which is relevant to your keyword. For example, our chocolate donuts article would at least link one time to a Wikipedia article about 'Chocolate Donuts'. Or a news article on the BBC website about 'chocolate donuts'.

Inbound link to another page on your own site

Interlinking is extremely powerful to help your other webpages on the same website giving each other a boost. Place at least one link to another page on your site in the content of your article. For example, if you have a related article on your site about 'vanilla donuts', link to that with the anchor text 'vanilla donuts'.

Image Alt Attribute(s)

You can at keywords to your on-page images that you embed in your content. These so-called 'alt attributes' can be placed using HTML, or in WordPress by changing the media content. Just place the exact match keyword ONLY ONCE in one of the images (so the alt-attribute will be 'chocolate-donuts' with a dash).

Embedded video (optional)

This will help boost your site even more, but is not necessary all the time. Embed a YouTube video with some traction (a bunch of views and interaction such as likes and comments) that contains your focus keyword. Preferably, this is an exact match keyword.

Body text keywords

Throughout your article, place the exact match keyword, but (very importantly) also variations of this keyword, in your overall text. The example image above shows exactly how to place these keywords throughout your text. It's very important to not force this placement, and simply write your text like a normal human being would. Just make sure you use your keyword at least once or twice. DO NOT overdo it, this will be seen as spam and will seriously harm your SEO for your page. Despite what some so-called experts claim, there is no real rule to when it is 'too much'. Just focus on providing value to your readers and don't spam your keyword, is the takeaway message here.

Relevant Factors Influencing On-Page SEO

There's a multitude of factors that will improve your website's SEO performance in Google's eyes. We will go over them one by one, and give a short explanation. As time progresses, these may become more or less important, as SEO is a dynamic thing, just like the internet itself.

Interlinking

This has already been touched upon, but it is very important to link between relevant pages on your own website quite often. This way, the link power will flow between the pages, making them stronger in the process. Google will see this as a positive thing and will consequently give you better rankings.

Website Speed

It's very important to keep track of the loadings speeds on your website. Logic tells us that better loading speeds of pages will give you better SEO results. Google provides website owners with a simple to use and understand free tool to track what to improve with regards to website speed. You can find the tool in the following URL (and simply enter your website domain name to get the results): https://developers.google.com/speed/pagespeed/insights/

Responsiveness

This basically boils down to the fact if your website design is suitable for mobile users. The internet is increasingly moving towards mobile platforms: smartphones and tablets. The majority of the traffic already comes from these sources and is only projected to grow. No wonder that Google deems it extremely important that your website design is 'responsive'. If it's not, fix it immediately. Not having a website design suited for mobile or tablet will completely obliterate your ranking results.

Safety

What's relatively new in the SEO space is the need for an SSL-certificate on your website. This is basically only visible in the domain URL – it will show an https://-

protocol instead of the regular http:// ones. Having an SSL is beneficial and will be increasingly important as time progresses. Not only for the privacy safety of your visitors, but also for SEO purposes. Your website host is able to give out an SSL-certificate for your site. Sometimes this will cost you a monthly or yearly fee, but in today's internet that's more than worth the investment to get that competitive edge from your competitors.

Website Age & Size

This one is difficult to influence and will come with time. The older and bigger the website, the more authority Google will give to it. As your site gets older it will collect more backlinks and more domain authority. That's also a reason why expired domains are so popular in the SEO space.

Topical Relevance

Having a very specific niche topic to your site, and sticking to that topic throughout your entire site, will be extremely helpful to determine what the site is about, and consequently will help you rank your site for niche keywords in your specific target market. Staying topically relevant and sticking to your topic is thus essential for some good old Google rankings.

Chapter 5: Link Building

Now that we have an overview of what will make the difference in on-page SEO performance, let's look at the invisible stuff: the off-page link building. Historically, the backlinks have always been the most important factor of ranking a website.

Google's algorithm has been built on understanding and giving value to backlinks from other websites, in order to determine which results should show up where for which search terms.

Why Numbers No Longer Matter

Until recently, it has been a common practice to, to say it bluntly, spam the shit out of a website in order to rank it. This no longer works. Over time Google has successfully changed its search algorithm to favor sites that have links pointing to them from websites that are authoritative and are visited by large numbers of people.

It is now common for new websites to rank high with only a few websites who point at them. These must be websites who are both authoritative and are relevant to the site that's getting ranked. You can't really rank a site about dog toys with an adult video site. Well, technically you could, but it's not very effective. It's preferable if you're making a site about dog toys, to get backlinks from already established websites about dogs or pets. The more QUALITY links you gather from other authority sites in your niche, the more likely it is you will show up for keywords in your website's niche.

Finding Quality Backlinks

Now, I can hear you ask: where do you get those links?! And my answer is simple: everywhere they are relevant. If you find an established website in your niche, go ahead and figure out how to get a link from them. Just don't go swapping links with website owners, because that's not beneficial to your SEO performance (anymore). In the world of SEO, we distinguish between the hats we put on when we are building links. We've got the white hat (the 'ethical') methods, and the black hat (the 'unethical' or cheating) methods. If it's a mix of the two, we call that a grey-hat link building method.

All of these methods work equally well, and both categories equally breach Google's Terms of Service. There's simply no way around that. If you are manipulating search results artificially, you are breaking Google's ToS. Google knows this, and Google accepts that SEO exists, despite being against the search results. Interestingly enough, Google's spokespersons have even spoken out about the fact that having SEO is actually beneficial to their overall search results. They also have a version of Google that does not have SEO in it (where SEO activities are filtered out), and the search results are actively worse than the 'real' results we get when searching for stuff in Google.

So do not be afraid when building links: you are breaking Google's terms of service, and Google is completely fine with that. If you do it ethically and will not try to 'break' the search results for your benefit. And yes, Black-Hat SEO can also be done in an ethical manner, believe it or not (this is obviously an opinion, but Black Hat backlinks are widely regarded as a sound method and are accepted among the SEO community).

Now that we've got the mandatory speech about breaking Terms of Service out of the way, let's look at the ways we can actually improve our rankings. Building quality links is what we are after. We do want as much backlinks as possible, but only from credible sources. Spamming sites with backlinks is a thing from the past. In fact, you should try purchasing 10.000 backlinks for $5 from Fiverr and see what it does to your search results. Exactly, you will get banished from the Google rankings. Or more likely, nothing will happen at all. So keep away from the shitty backlinks and start building links to your site manually. It's completely fine to outsource, but for the love of all that is good and holy, please only purchase links that are proven to work for SEO purposes. And never purchase backlinks if you don't know what you're doing yet.

Okay, now I've discouraged you enough to get you back to reality. So, let's look at what we _can_ do to improve our website's visibility. How do we build high quality manual backlinks that will give us good SEO results? Here's what the real SEO's are doing to achieve results.

White-Hat Methods

Guest Posting

This is the most common white-hat method that provides value to your site. You will create an engaging piece of content that is well-written on someone else's website. Preferably, this is an authority in your niche that will give you a powerful backlink!

Guest posting means you have the ability to tap into a new audience on someone else's website that already has traffic. You help build their site by giving them an article that their readers enjoy, and in return you can get one or two backlinks. One will be a branded URL (your website URL – learn more about this in the next chapter of this book), and if possible try to sneak in at least one keyword specific anchor text (again, please refer to the next chapter to understand what this is).

It's very important that you do not link to this article on your own site, because that would nullify the SEO power of it. Google regards backlinks from authority websites that point to your website, but you NOT pointing back to that site, as the most powerful.

Press Releases

A classic way to gather mass backlinks is to do a Press
Release. If you have some news or a big launch on your
site, put out a press release. Even it if doesn't get picked
up, a lot of automatic press release sites will embed the
article on their site. This will give you heaps of good
backlinks. A sound method to get a lot of backlinks fast.
They may not all be that powerful, though. So don't expect
a miracle after releasing one press release article.

Organic Shares (Have Quality Content)

It seems so logical, and I encourage any website builder to
do this anyways, but organic shares still work magic. Have
AMAZING content that is unique and encourages shares.
This includes social media shares, but preferably shares
from established websites. Having them mention you
organically in their articles is the most optimal way to get a
bunch of high quality backlinks to your website.

Submitting Links Yourself

Some websites allow you to actually submit a link to your
site for nothing in return. Find these sites and go ahead
and make a link for yourself! Especially powerful for local
SEO citations (see Chapter 7). Most sites that allow you to
do this are databases or directory sites. Avoid directory

sites that ask you for a link in return like the plague, it will not help you rank that much at all.

Outreach (Asking for a Backlink)

The classic method of asking for a favor. Very important is that you do NOT do link swapping, that will hurt both your site's SEO. Simply notifying a website owner or author about a piece of content on your site will get you a lot of good backlink results. This goes back to making god, high quality content. If it's relevant and share-worthy, a webmaster will be happy to give you a link for free.

Usually, this method works best if sites already have an article about a certain topic that's also on your website. Notify them that you help them improve that article by including a link to a piece of your own content. And boom! Free backlink.

Sneaky tip: Use a software like Xenu Link Sleuth (free to download online) to uncover broken links on relevant websites. If you find one, make a piece of content on exactly what that link was referring to. Notify the webmaster that they have a broken link on their site and that your content can help replace that link. They will almost always be happy to fix it, especially if you explain that having a broken link on their site is bad for their Google rankings (because that's actually the case).

Black-Hat Methods

Private Blog Network (PBN)

The most important black hat SEO method is the creation of a Private blog Network (PBN). This basically means you will go ahead and purchase a whole bunch of powerful expired domain names and create real websites on them that link back to your 'money site' (also known as the site you are trying to rank). Having a PBN is a quick way to generate a boost towards your search engine rankings.

However, it does require a significant time and money investment, thus it is only a good option if you are knowledgeable at what you are doing. You do need to learn from an expert how to build PBN's. Otherwise you will either shoot yourself in the foot building a PBN, or will have no idea where to even begin.

Simple steps you need to take:

- Find niche-relevant expired domains with 13+ Trust Flow and 15+ Citation Flow, at LEAST 10 referring domains, and a clean non-spammy anchor text (use Majestic).

- Register the domain using WhoIS domain protection OR using fake login details (this is why this method is considered 'black hat')
- Get a separate hosting account (for each PBN site) under a fake name and if possible use CloudFlare to diminish your PBN footprint.
- Create your website with as little similarities to each other as possible. Create articles on these powerful domains with backlinks to your 'money site' (the site you are trying to rank).
- Backlinks should have good anchor text (see next chapter) and should only have 3 links maximum per PBN to your money site.

Needless to say, using this method requires some training and management. It will also cost you a lot of money. Investing in a PBN is, however extremely powerful for ranking purposes if you are doing things correctly. But you NEED training on this, otherwise I guarantee you will not succeed and will get your site penalized by Google.

Reducing your PBN footprint is the core difficulty in having a PBN network, apart from the many hosting companies, alias names, and large monetary investment. The method is strictly forbidden by Google, that's why it is a black hat method. However, I know for a fact pretty much every self-proclaimed SEO expert uses a PBN to some degree. Why? Because it works. And it works fast. If you do it correctly, that is.

Buying Backlinks

Commonplace in SEO, but strictly forbidden by Google. Exchange money for rankings is not only technically forbidden by Google, it can be dangerous. You do not have control over your links, even if they come from someone else's PBN. Good backlinks can be found on marketplaces like Konker.io, or PBN Butler.

Fiverr also has a few but they also have extremely terrible ones. You want to look for manual link building. I do not encourage you to buy links, I am just letting you know that this exists. It is strictly forbidden by Google, thus another Black Hat SEO method.

Chapter 6: Anchor Text

One of the most important aspects about understanding off-page SEO, is having an understanding of what anchor text is and how it can help you rank your website. We will go over both topics and hopefully you will understand the concept a bit better.

What is Anchor Text?

We all know what it is, because if you ever browsed the internet you've seen them. Anchor texts are basically those little clickable words in an article, which will bring you to another page or website. We can implement these clickable words using HTML code (or by simply adding a link in your text in WordPress):

ANCHOR TEXT

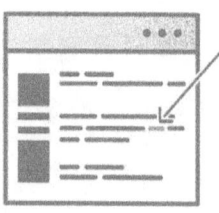

<p> dolor sit amet, ad per probo partiendo, pro te graeco cotidieque. Nemore quodsi scaevola te ninja, eirmod aliquid epicuri <a href="http://website.com">click here</a> mei cu, fabulas accusam epicurei ex vix. Congue primis posidonium ad est, ne per altera dicunt. Et ius facer temporibus, sea veniam salutatus interesset. Nonumy inimicus similique an eam, et eum populo volumus. Mea et veri lorem invenire, iudico labitur efficiantur qui no. Tritani aliquid honestatis ne sea, ea cum </p>

link on a page   link in code

Quite literally, the exact wording which you can click on is what we need for ranking our site in Google. For example, if I have a bakery website, I want an authority website about baking bread to link to my site using the word I want to show up for in Google, let's say: chocolate donuts. So in the ideal situation, I want that authority site about baking to link to my site using a clickable keyword 'chocolate donuts'.

In the image above, the anchor text is 'click here'. If this clickable word world link to your website, your site will actually have a chance of ranking for the keyword 'click here'. So whatever that clickable word is that links to your site, you will have a chance to show up for in Google.

Obviously, you want to show up for low competition keywords in your niche. So that's what you try to achieve when you are interacting with other website owners to get backlinks.

A guest post would ideally include 'chocolate donuts' as clickable word to your site, as well as your website URL. A Private Blog Network (PBN) article would work the same.

There's three types of anchor text:
- **Branded:** This includes your website URL, or a variation of your brand name. At least a significant

portion of all the links pointing to your site should contain branded anchor text.

- **Non-branded:** These are the exact match words that we just talked about. Ideally, these should be the keywords you want to show up for in Google. These are basically all anchor texts that are not the website URL variations, or company brand name. You could have other brand names here, which still counts as 'non-branded'. Branded anchor text in SEO terms basically means your website brand name.

- **Misc:** Everything that's not text or URL's. Links within images, terms like 'click here', arrow symbols, other obscure symbols or numbers, anything that's not a search term, URL of your own site, or a variation of the name of your brand or site URL.

How Anchor Text Helps You Rank

Simply put, the website which has the most QUALITY backlinks with keyword specific anchor text will show up first in Google for that specific keyword (or keyword variation). There's however a very thin line between using 'too much' non-branded anchor texts with only 1 keyword in it and using 'exactly the right amount' of them.

As a rule of thumb, you want to do a little dance around your target anchor text, ideally. This is what we refer to as the SEO dance. Basically, it means you build only 2-3 exact match keyword anchor texts to your site, and a LOT (just as much as you need to rank for your keyword) of anchor text that partially contains that targeted keyword, or uses synonyms. This is called anchor text diversification.

Anchor Text Diversification

As an example of an ideal anchor text situation, we take our chocolate donuts ranking. For our example, we assume that all backlinks have equally powerful effect on your site. Then what we would want is 10 sites to have a non-branded anchor text to our site with the following anchor text diversification:

- Chocolate donuts (2x)
- Pure chocolate donut (1x)
- Donut Chocolate flavor (1x)
- Delicious donuts (1x)
- Chocolate baked goodies (1x)
- White choco donut (1x)
- Pure donut choco flavor (1x)
- Nutella organic donut (1x)
- Special chocolatey treats (1x)

And the list could be as creative and big as you would like. The SEO dance basically is that you include a part of the desired keyword, but not the exact keyword in its entirety. We only do this to avoid any trouble with Google. If you're unsure about the anchor text of your own website, go to http://www.majestic.com and check the pie chart of your current state of business. If a lot of non-branded anchor texts pops up, it's time to gather more diverse backlinks as quickly as possible.

Too much of the exact same anchor keywords can very quickly result in a penalty by Google. Google sees something like that very quickly as spamming a keyword. This could result in your site being marked as a spam site, and it could even get de-indexed, which means it will completely be removed from Google search all together. So be aware of this before you start building backlinks, yet do not let it frighten you. If you follow the example, you will most likely be completely safe.

Chapter 7: Local SEO Essentials

A specific subcategory of SEO, but one that's very profitable for local businesses, is called local SEO. Basically, this means that in your keywords you also have included a geographic location, such as a city, region, state, province or even suburb and ZIP code. For these search terms, Google shows maps of relevant companies in the specific area. These maps and attached companies are called 'local snack pack'.

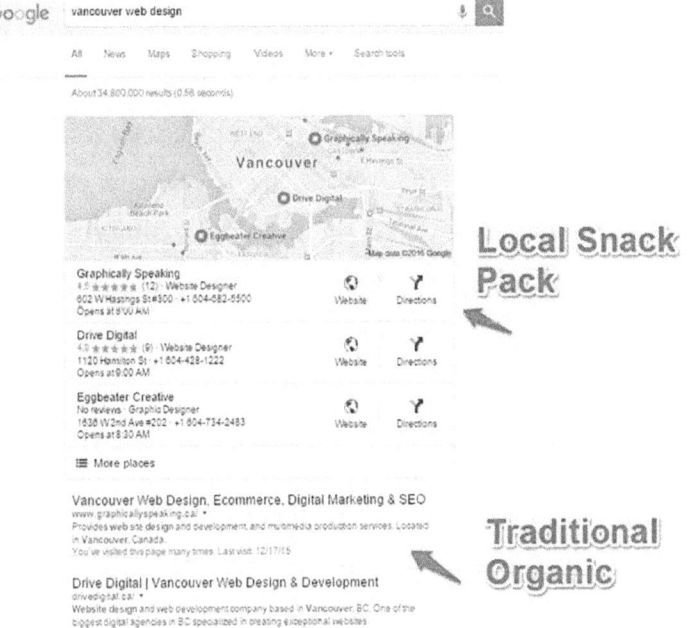

111

The list of companies always used to be around 7 in total, but has since been reduced to a maximum of three companies. As a company, you really want to be in the top 3 search results for that specific reason. There's a few strategies you should employ to achieve this. This chapter will go over the most relevant factors to rank high for local SEO search terms. This overview is not meant as a guide on local SEO, which could be a completely separate book entirely. We go over three of the most essential things you should do.

Verify Business Ownership

If you haven't done so already, verify that you own your business over at https://www.google.com/business/. Here you can claim your Google 'My Business'-page. Simply fill in the details as precise as possible, and place relevant keywords in the description. Choosing correct categories and uploading at least 5 good photo's is very important to optimize your page (and optimize your local SEO performance).

Google Reviews

This may seem extremely logical, but there's literally thousands of businesses that aren't even looking at this. However, having loads of 4 or 5 star Google reviews will drastically improve your ability to show up in the local search results. It's very simple: the business with the most reviews that are positive, wins the local ranking game.

Actively ask your customers to leave reviews when they had a good experience. Offer them discounts, rewards or other benefits to do this. Your investment will be worth it ten times over. Because having good Google results is worth thousands of dollars monthly, if not millions, depending on the business you are in. Do not underestimate the power of local business rankings for your business success. Local SEO is an easy way to make your company visible to targeted, local (!) customers.

Local Citations

Your company is likely to already have a few citations, but there's an opportunity to optimize this even further. Citations are basically mentions of your company website (and social media profiles) in directories such as Yellow Pages, Yelp, and so much more. A full list of category-specific websites to place citations can be found at https://moz.com/learn/local/citations-by-category/. More citations equals higher local rankings, simple.

Chapter 8: Search Engine Optimization Tips

Coming to the final chapters of this short instructional book on search engine optimization, I want to leave you with a few useful tips & tricks that will help you propel your website forward. From experience, these are the key elements that helped me give my own SEO operations a boost. Here they are.

Tip #1: Social Media matters

It's no surprise that social media is an important factor within the rankings of Google. Without social media, our webspace looked completely different. But now that we have things like Facebook and Twitter, it's best to use them to our advantage. And by that I mean, gain backlinks from them, and not waste your time posting cat pictures or nonsensical stuff that won't get your results.

Focus on your site, not your Twitter account. And if possible automate these social media systems as much as possible. The key is to use them for backlinks, not to waste your time on!

Tip #2: Go mobile or go bankrupt

In 2017 and beyond, having a responsive website is no longer optional. It is an absolute must. Over 70% of Google's internet traffic comes from mobile devices these days (either tablets or mobile phones), and the numbers are rising every day. Therefore it's only natural that Google adapts to this trend by favoring websites that are mobile friendly.

For the website you wish to rank in Google, you must perform what is known as a 'responsiveness check'. This basically means seeing if your website is fit for the many types of mobile devices out there. The process is extremely simple, copy your website URL and go to: http://responsivedesignchecker.com/. Congrats if your website passed this basic test. If it didn't it's time to contact your web designer for an update to your site. Google will literally throw your site into the search rankings dumpster if you cannot pass this basic test.

Tip #3: Build new sites on high-metrics expired domains

There's a simple reason why the market for buying expired domains is flourishing. The main reason being the metrics that are attached to these expired domain names. Simply visit GoDaddy Auctions and see for yourself for how much some domains go.

Not only will you be able to pick up some cool names, looking out for domains with high domain and page power (which are metrics that are retained when a domain expires) are something to look out for.

Tip #4: Get SSL security for your site

The new safety standard will become ever more important in the upcoming time. For a while now, Google favors websites that have an SSL certificate attached to their site. This will certainly impact your rankings and give you that slight edge over your competition.

An SSL certificate can be easily detected by the "https://"-protocol used on your site. If your website does not display this protocol, your website is not SSL-protected. An SSL-certificate can be purchased (or sometimes even obtained for free) from your website hosting provider. Usually, your host will ask a small monthly or annual fee for having an SSL certificate. A basic SSL "https://"-protocol will suffice for SEO purposes.

Tip #5: Outsource the tedious and repetitive tasks

The only way you can focus on creating the best possible website there is, is to actually go ahead and outsource most of the tedious little tasks that come with performing SEO yourself. This will be the only way for you to scale up your online business and actually get some success.

Time is your most precious resource, and the only thing to replace that is money: use your money as an investment to leverage your time wisely. Again, 20% of your actions will generate 80% of the results. Let the other 80% of work be done by hard workers that you have employed.

Go to an outsourcing website such as Upwork and hire some writers, for example. It's really not that much of a money investment as you would think, and it will free up an amazing amount of time for you to do more important tasks.

Tip #6: Don't get lost in the details

There's many small tasks or manual link building to get lost in when you're doing SEO. Don't fall into the trap of getting lost in the details. As you outsource more and more small tasks, you can free up your time to focus on the content of your site and not so much on the SEO side of things.

Again, 80% of the results are achieved by doing 20% of the work. So choose your tasks, and let others do the time consuming stuff. I cannot stress the importance of this enough. If you want to be successful fast, at least.

Tip #7: Silo structure your website

I highly recommend if you're targeting categories or geo-locations, that you look into a website 'silo-structure'. This means, creating a hierarchy of interlinked webpages on your site. For our baker example, the hierarchy could be:

1. Bakery in Canada
2. Bakery Specialties
3. Donuts
4. Chocolate Donuts
5. Pure Chocolate Donuts

All layers of categories would have their own page, linking to a list of subcategories. This will allow link-power to effectively flow throughout your entire website. The URL structure then could look like the following (when targeting pure chocolate donuts in Canada bakeries):
http://marysbakery.com/canada/bakery-specialties/donuts/chocolate/pure-chocolate/.

Tip #8: Be aware of changes in the algorithm

The internet is always changing, and so will the Google search algorithm. Already there's a trend going on that mobile and social signals will be more and more important. As the internet develops itself, this will continue to change continuously. Do not get discouraged by this fact, but use it to your advantage! Stay ahead of the curve by constantly adapting to the newest trends on the web. Does a new social media platform emerge? Get on it. Will Google focus more and more on topical relevance? Build your links only to sites that are very relevant to your niche, before the new rules kick in. This way you will eventually become the king of the hill, even though you might not be that right now.

Tip #9: Don't put your eggs in one basket

Google is by far the most important player in the search engine world, but there's more than just Google on this planet. Think for example about Microsoft's search engine Bing. Or even Yahoo's search engine AltaVista. People actually use all of these tools to find information on the web, believe it or not. All search engines work in a slightly different manner, so it's a good idea to look into some of the other search engines as well.

Another way to look at this tip is to not have 'just' a single website. Putting all your income risk into a single website is a recipe for disaster, income-wise. Always have more than one site that makes you money if that's your core business and core income strategy. If you find a niche that works, by all means go ahead and dominate the keywords of that particular niche. Make 2, 3 or even 5 websites that are about the exact same topic. If it has proven to make you good money, why not multiple that income? Simply apply the exact same SEO linking strategy too all websites, heck, even give them the same type of content and layout. It's all perfectly fine in Google's eyes. They do not care that much who owns the sites. Google only cares about if the content is good and if people enjoy that content (visitor retention statistics).

Tip #10: Be patient and persistent

Building up your website takes time and effort, there is no doubt about that. Mark your goal and identify the steps needed to get there. Every day, make a list of tasks to do in order to get there. Work off your list every single day and you will have certain success. No website is going to skyrocket in a week or even in a month. If you cannot see results, it means you need to keep building content and keep building quality backlinks to your website. There's no hack to becoming successful.

Tip #11: Look beyond just SEO

SEO is just one strategy to generate traffic to your website. Using this together with a sound social media presence will likely propel your site even further into the top of Google. Knowing that paid traffic can also give your site a good boost, especially when you're running some type of campaign, is important within your success story. Don't be afraid to implement strategies beyond SEO, even if it is your main, number one strategy for traffic generation.

It might seem silly to invest in Google AdWords advertising when you are trying to put effort and money into organic search, but it will be worth it in the shorter term, or for related keywords that you do not yet rank for. And Facebook users will not see your Google results, so by all means go ahead and specialize yourself in Facebook Advertisements. More sources of traffic means more prospects that are willing to buy from you, and in the end will result in an increased income level for your websites.

Chapter 9: Parting Words

It will take time and a lot of effort to create a good SEO performance for your site. There's a lot to it, but do not get overwhelmed or discouraged by what you have learned in this short guidebook. Whilst it will help to implement all of this into your website(s), it's certainly not always required to do it absolutely perfectly.

The thing is, your direct competition for the search terms you are trying to rank for is facing the same challenges. And no single site or SEO performance is perfect. So you don't have to be perfect in your SEO either. Set your goal to beat your competition's performance, do not set your goal to be perfect in SEO.

Becoming number 1 in Google means to be better than the rest, it absolutely does not mean you need to be perfect in applying all the SEO rules and tricks. Always remember this when you are into SEO rankings. Hopefully, this short guidebook has given you some more in-depth insight into the topic, and will lead you on a path towards a successful, SEO-optimized website. A path that will not be without obstacles, but certainly a path that will be worthwhile, and in the end will be very profitable indeed.

If you are unsure how to start with SEO effectively, I highly recommend you to create a WordPress-based website. There's heaps of very effective tools for this website building framework that will propel your site building efforts forward much faster. I speak from experience when I say that ALL people that have SEO businesses prefer WordPress sites, for their ease of use.

Hopefully you are now a little bit more knowledgeable on the topic and will be able to start focusing on ranking your site, and providing the best possible content to your readers. Because, yes, it also matters for SEO purposes how long people will stay on your site.

When you build your site and do SEO, please put your effort into the most important tasks that will bring your result, and outsource what you can afford. All the best in your online journey, and my gratitude for giving me the opportunity to get you on your way with your project!

www.ingramcontent.com/pod-product-compliance
Lightning Source LLC
Chambersburg PA
CBHW070041210526
45170CB00012B/556